The Destroyer of Worlds

Oppenheimer

and the Atomic Bomb

Written by Rod Smith
and illustrated by Derry Dillon

Published 2024
Poolbeg Press Ltd

123 Grange Hill, Baldoyle
Dublin 13, Ireland

A catalogue record for this book is available from the British Library.

ISBN 978 1 78199 684 3

1

Cover design and illustrations by Derry Dillon
Printed by GPS Colour Graphics Ltd

To
Denise, Alex & Oisín

With Special Thanks to
Jazz O'Brien and Mark Stanley

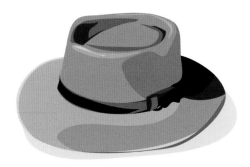

J. Robert Oppenheimer

Date of Birth: 22nd April 1904

Place of Birth: New York City, USA

Died: 18th February 1967

Place of Death: Princeton, New Jersey, USA

Oppenheimer's Childhood

"Why do I have to wear a suit to dinner?" eight-year-old Robert Oppenheimer asked his Irish nanny, Nellie Connolly.

"Your father insists on it, sir!" Nellie laughed as she adjusted his jacket.

"That's right, Nellie!" Robert's father agreed as he entered the room.

It was 1912 and Robert lived with his family in a very fancy apartment in Manhattan, New York City.

"We must dress the part!" his father said. "You are a lucky child! Not everyone has a cook, servants and a chauffeur!"

"Or a nanny!" Nellie joked as she brushed Robert's hair.

"Perhaps young Robert will be an artist like me when he grows up?" his mother Ella suggested as she popped her head around the door.

Robert's father nodded. "If that is what he wants! With excellence and purpose, Robert can achieve anything! I was born in Germany and came to the United States in 1888. I had no money, no education and I could not speak English. Now look at me today! I have a successful business. Tell me, Robert, why am I successful?"

Robert smiled. He had been asked this many times before. The answer was always the same. "Because you worked with excellence and purpose!"

"Precisely!"

Nellie fetched a tissue to wipe Robert's runny nose.

Ella looked alarmed. "Are you catching a cold, Robert?" she asked anxiously.

"I'm fine, Mother! You're always worried about me!"

"That's what mothers do!" she replied.

Robert was a very bright student at school. He loved poetry, reading and writing. His favourite hobby was collecting and classifying rocks. (His grandfather gave him a box of rock samples when he was younger). He joined the New York Mineralogical Club when he was eleven. A year later, he gave a speech about rocks to the members of the club. The audience were amazed that he was so young!

Robert graduated from school after getting top marks in English, Maths, Physics, Greek, Latin, French and German. That summer he travelled to Europe with his parents for a holiday and became very ill. He came back to America to recover, spending time in New Mexico (in the southwestern part of the United States) and riding horses there. As he travelled through New Mexico with a schoolteacher friend, he discovered the secluded Los Alamos Ranch School. Twenty years later this would be the location used to develop the first atomic bomb under his leadership.

The College Years

Robert enrolled at Harvard College in 1922. At first, he studied chemistry. Then he moved on to physics. He loved his time there. "I devoured knowledge," he said later. "I had a real chance to learn." He took on Latin and Greek as extra subjects and finished the whole course in three years instead of four. Interesting scientific discoveries were being made in Europe at this time, so once he completed his course he decided to study next at Cambridge University in England.

Robert was now smoking cigarettes and wasn't eating properly. Toast with peanut butter and chocolate syrup was his regular lunch!

He was not very good at laboratory experiments in the university. He kept getting them wrong! One day he became so annoyed he put chemicals into an apple and left it on his tutor's desk! The apple was never eaten but the college did find out what Robert had done. His parents were visiting England at the time, so they were called in to discuss the matter. Robert was given another chance to continue his studies and he finished his course without any further incidents.

In 1926, Robert moved to Germany to study. He worked hard and enjoyed his time there. He got on very well with the students and was very confident in class. Sometimes he would interrupt the tutors and correct them (in German) if he felt they were making mistakes! At exam time, one of his tutors joked that Robert knew more about the subject than the tutor himself did! Robert continued his interest in poetry and had a poem called "Crossing" published in 1928.

By the time he finished his studies, Robert had written lots of scientific papers. One of his later articles predicted the discovery of black holes in the universe. He travelled to the Netherlands and gave a lecture to the students in Dutch! He had taught himself the language. The students liked him so much they gave him a nickname "Opje", a shortened version of his surname.

From 1929 Robert was teaching full-time in two universities in California: the University of California (Berkeley) and the California Institute of Technology (Caltech). At first his classes were very difficult to understand because the subjects were very complicated. One day a professor from the college sat in on Robert's class. After the class, the professor said, "Robert, that was a beautiful lecture, but I must admit I didn't understand a word of it!" Other times the students couldn't hear what he said because he spoke in a very soft voice. "Speak up!" they sometimes had to call out!

Robert's classes began to improve and soon he became so popular that students would travel from all over the country to hear him. He always tried to be helpful. He would meet the students in groups or invite them out to dinner at his house or at restaurants, where he would pay the bill. Sometimes the students were served hot chili by Robert at mealtime and needed to drink lots of water! When a student was having a problem, Robert would encourage the other students to help. Sometimes he would change his lectures during the class if he saw that someone was having trouble understanding the topic. His students adapted his Dutch nickname "Opje" and started to call him "Oppie" as a term of affection. They even began to copy how he dressed and how he spoke and acted!

After the crash of the Wall Street Stock Market in 1929, times were very tough for people all around the world. In America, the following years were known as "The Great Depression". Jobs were extremely hard to find, and many people did not have a place to live or enough food to eat. Many Americans were attracted to the Communist Party at the time as they thought it promoted the idea that everything should be shared equally. (The Communist Party controlled the Soviet Union, under the leadership of Joseph Stalin but people there were not actually treated equally.) Robert's brother Frank was a Communist Party member. During this time, Robert became closely involved with Jean Tatlock who was studying to be a psychiatrist and wrote for a Communist Party newspaper.

The Manhattan Project

Some philosophers and scientists in ancient times suggested that everything in the universe is made up of tiny particles. The ancient Greeks called them "atomos". But it was not until the 19th and 20th centuries that scientists discovered that atoms are made up of smaller particles called electrons, protons and neutrons. Scientists wondered if it would be possible to "split" the atom into smaller pieces. Scientists called this "nuclear fission". They realised this could create huge amounts of energy which could be used to generate power or create a bomb. In 1938 "splitting" the atom was completed successfully in an experiment in Germany. When the Second World War broke out in 1939, it was feared that the Nazis would create a powerful new "atomic" weapon using this new knowledge. (Robert helped some Jewish families escape from the Nazis in the late 1930s and arranged for them to come to America. His own family were Jewish.)

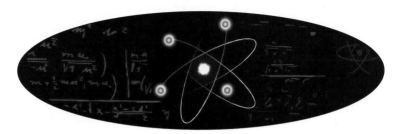

Albert Einstein, the famous scientist, and others wrote a letter to American President Roosevelt. Even though the United States was not involved in the war, Einstein urged President Roosevelt to create the atomic bomb before the Nazis had an opportunity to do so. President Roosevelt agreed. (After the war, when it was discovered that the Nazis had never been close to making such a bomb, Einstein called the letter one of the biggest mistakes of his life.)

The 7th of December 1941was a date that President Roosevelt claimed would "live in infamy" after Japan attacked the American naval base at Pearl Harbour, Hawaii, killing thousands of people. The United States of America was now at war.

The Manhattan Project was created. Brigadier General Leslie Groves was in charge. By 1944 almost 130,000 people across the country were working on trying to create an atomic bomb. Brigadier General Groves asked Robert to take charge of the secret weapons laboratory which would create the actual bomb.

Not everyone supported this move. A friend of Robert commented that Robert "was a very impractical fellow. He walked about with scuffed shoes and a funny hat, and he didn't know anything about equipment". One other criticism of Robert was that he had no experience managing large groups of people. Others thought he was a communist because of his friendships in the past. However, Brigadier General Groves believed that Robert was the ideal choice to lead the team of scientists because he was "a real genius who knows about everything".

To preserve the secrecy of the Manhattan Project, Robert suggested locating the laboratory on the site of the Los Alamos Ranch school, which he had visited twenty years earlier in New Mexico. Houses were built there for the scientists and their families. Servants were also provided to help with housework. A school was built, along with a library, a post office, a radio station, restaurants and a small hospital. There was even a town council!

Robert lived at Los Alamos with his wife Kitty and son Peter. They later had a daughter, Katherine. Everyone recognised Robert. He was tall and thin and usually wore jeans or khaki trousers and a blue shirt. He normally wore a porkpie hat on his head. If he was not smoking a cigarette, he would be smoking a pipe. This gave him a very bad cough which stayed with him for the rest of his days.

Even though there was tight security at Los Alamos, Robert insisted that the scientists within the facility should be allowed to talk to one another freely and share ideas. Robert was friendly and persuasive. He would arrange regular meetings, observe experiments, and encourage open discussions. When a scientist asked Robert if creating an atomic bomb was the right thing to do, Robert replied "What if the Nazis get it first?" The Nazis had developed a rocket called a V2 and the allies feared that a nuclear warhead could be applied to it. Scientists from Britain were flown in to help in the effort to create a bomb. They had been working on a similar secret project called "Tube Alloys" without success. Now they combined their efforts with those of Robert's team.

Some scientists worried about the impact of the explosion on the planet.

"If an atomic bomb explodes it could set the whole atmosphere of the earth on fire," one scientist suggested.

"This is very unlikely – I have done the calculations," another replied. "There is almost no chance that this will happen."

"Almost no chance? So, there is a tiny chance?"

"A tiny chance, but very unlikely!"

Robert continued to encourage the scientists to work on producing the bomb.

While he worked at Los Alamos, complaints were still being made that Robert was too close to the communists and could not be trusted. It was claimed that he might be passing on secrets to the Soviet Union. Brigadier General Groves continued to support Robert and insisted that he was the right person to be in charge.

The scientists at Los Alamos had a working version of an atomic bomb ready in July 1945. The war in Europe was over after the surrender of the Nazis. However, the war with Japan continued.

Brigadier Groves told Robert that the test would have to be completed by 16th July. The new American President Harry S. Truman was going to an important conference in Germany the following day. He had to know if the bomb would work!

On Sunday 15th July, everyone was ready for what Robert had named the "Trinity" test, in the New Mexico desert. Robert was so nervous he drank lots of cups of black coffee and kept smoking cigarettes. Despite the appearance of a huge storm, the weather finally cleared.

The countdown began. All the scientists were worried. Could the storm have damaged the bomb? What if the bomb exploded and set fire to the atmosphere? What if it did not explode after all? The seconds counted down. 5 … 4 … 3 … 2 …1… It was now or never! The controls were activated. The dark sky turned white, then yellow, orange and red. This was followed by intense heat and a very loud bang. Energy equal to thousands of tons of dynamite produced a fallout cloud that looked like a large mushroom. The fireball produced could be seen hundreds of miles away.

Everyone cheered. Robert was relieved. "I guess it worked," he said to his brother Frank who was standing near him.

Years later, when Robert was asked to recall his thoughts about that night, he said the lines from a sacred Hindu text came into his head: *"Now I am become Death, the Destroyer of Worlds."*

At the conference in Germany, President Truman was delighted. He told the British Prime Minister Churchill about the success of the atomic bomb test. While Robert hoped that the news would be shared with the Soviets, President Truman only told Stalin that "a new weapon of unusual destructive force" had been created.

"That Awful Thing" – Picking Bombing Targets

Robert was now involved in discussions with politicians, scientists and military personnel to decide where and when the bomb should be used.

President Truman wanted the war to end quickly without the loss of more American soldiers. He was told that the Japanese would not surrender even though most of their army, navy and air force had been destroyed. Their leader, Emperor Hirohito, was adored by the Japanese public and they would fight for him until the end. A plan to invade Japan by land had been prepared but it was accepted that many people on both sides would be killed in the fighting.

"Can we drop a bomb in an unpopulated area to give the Japanese a warning?" one politician asked.

"We cannot give a warning. What if it doesn't explode? It must be a surprise," one of the senior generals, General MacArthur, replied. "We only have a small number of bombs ready to go. We must use them in the most effective way."

"The Soviet Union is going to enter the war on our side on 15th August," another politician remarked. "What if they invade parts of the Far East and decide to stay there permanently?"

"Perhaps we need to finish this war before 15th August then!"

Some scientists protested: "We created these bombs to stop the Nazis. Nobody ever mentioned bombing Japan. If we use these bombs against Japan, it will be one of the greatest blunders of history."

The Supreme Commander of the Allied Forces, General Eisenhower, thought the Japanese were ready to surrender and should not be hit with that "awful thing". Robert did not learn this until after the war, leading him to conclude that "the bombing in Hiroshima may have been a tragic mistake".

President Truman ordered the bombing to proceed. "This is the greatest thing in history," he said. "We need to drop these bombs to end this war once and for all."

Four cities were chosen as possible targets – Kyoto, Hiroshima, Kokura, and Niigata. Then Kyoto was removed and replaced by Nagasaki.

On the 6th of August 1945, the crew of the B-29 bomber the *Enola Gay* completed their six-hour flight from a small island called Tinian in the Pacific Ocean. Their destination: Hiroshima. Their captain, Colonel Paul W. Tibbets, asked the crew to write letters to their families just in case they did not make it back safely. Only a small number on board knew what the actual mission was. Many of the people in Hiroshima ignored the plane when it appeared and did not take shelter. What possible damage could one plane do to an entire city? (When other Japanese cities had been bombed in the past there were hundreds of planes involved.)

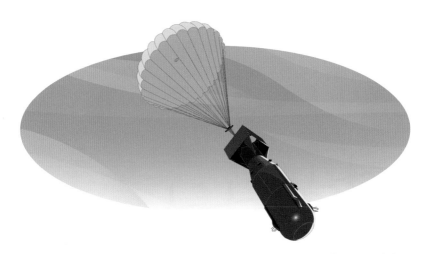

At 8.15 a.m. the bomb *Little Boy* was dropped by parachute over a city centre bridge. It fell slowly through the air and exploded, as planned, above the city. A mushroom cloud was followed by a brilliant flash of light. This was followed by a loud booming sound.

"My God, what have we done?" one of the crew of the *Enola Gay* asked as they flew away from the scene of devastation.

Almost 70,000 were estimated to have died instantly. Many more died afterwards. Huge parts of the city were destroyed.

News of Hiroshima reached Robert and the scientists at Los Alamos. At an assembly that evening, Robert stood on a stage in front of everyone, holding his hands up together like a boxer who had won a fight. Everyone was cheering.

"While it is too early to determine the results of the bombing, I am sure the Japanese didn't like it!" he shouted. *"My only regret is that we did not get a chance to use it against the Germans!"*

Despite the destructive power of this new weapon, Japan still did not surrender. The order was given to drop a second bomb. In the early-morning darkness of the 9th of August, a plane called *Bockscar*, carrying the bomb *Fat Man*, waited on the runway of Tinian Island. The destination was the city of Kokura. The pilot was Irish American Major Charles W. Sweeney. The plane began to taxi down the runway and picked up speed as it prepared to take to the air.

"Someone has turned off the lights at the end of the runway!" one of the crew shouted. *"We can't see where it ends!"*

Major Sweeney continued to accelerate in the darkness. He knew if they crashed the bomb would detonate, destroying the plane and probably the whole island. He managed to get the plane into the air just seconds before it plunged into the Pacific Ocean!

Visibility at Kokura was poor – the sky was full of clouds. As the crew couldn't see the target, Major Sweeney altered course to the back-up target. Kokura was saved. The city of Nagasaki would not be so fortunate. It is estimated that 40,000 people were killed on the day. Many more died in the following months from injuries and radiation sickness.

On 14th August 1945, despite attempts by some young Japanese officers to take over the government and continue the war, Japan formally surrendered after a radio broadcast from Emperor Hirohito himself. (This was the first time the Japanese people had ever heard his voice.) The Second World War was over.

The mood in Los Alamos was different this time. Nobody cheered or celebrated. "The atomic bomb is so terrible a weapon that war is now impossible," Robert said. "If these weapons are used in the future, then the time will come when all people will curse the name of Los Alamos."

After the Bomb

Robert called for a ban on the use of nuclear weapons. He met American President Truman to discuss the issue.

"Mr President, I feel I have blood on my hands," he told the president.

"The blood is on my hands. You let me worry about that!" the president angrily responded.

After the meeting, the president was very annoyed. "He doesn't have half as much blood on his hands as I have. You just don't go around bellyaching about it! Do not let that cry-baby scientist in here ever again!" he ordered.

Robert soon became a celebrity when people learned about Los Alamos. He was regarded as the "Father of the Atomic Bomb" and was interviewed in the famous publications and media outlets of the time.

Robert began to use his new-found fame to argue against the use of the bomb which he now called "a most terrible weapon". He believed that the newly formed United Nations had a key role to play in making sure that a nuclear arms race (where countries would compete to create nuclear weapons) did not take place.

After Los Alamos, Robert went back to teaching in California. In 1947 Lewis Strauss offered him the role of Director of the Institute for Advanced Study in Princeton, New Jersey. Albert Einstein, who lived there, described it as a place for "people who are trying to think". Scientists from all over the world were invited to spend some time there and were inspired by Robert to make discoveries in the world of physics. Dr. Sheila Power from Galway studied there while Robert was in charge.

Robert became a senior member of the Atomic Energy Commission which kept a close eye on nuclear research and the development of nuclear weapons. When scientists wanted to create an even more powerful hydrogen bomb, Robert did not support it, "How many more weapons do we need?" he asked.

Investigations

The FBI had always been keeping a close eye on Robert since the 1930s as they suspected he might be a Communist supporter. When he was in charge at Los Alamos he was regularly followed by FBI agents. They opened any letters he received in the post, monitored his phone calls, and planted electronic hearing devices (bugs) in his office and home. Even Robert's driver worked as an FBI informant!

After the war the FBI director J. Edgar Hoover accused Robert of being a member of the Communist Party. He even suggested (without proof) that Robert was going to defect to the Soviet Union! The FBI continued to illegally bug his phones and follow his every move. Robert and his family knew they were being monitored. One day Robert was on the phone to his wife Kitty when they heard a clicking sound on the telephone line. "I wonder who is listening to us?" Robert asked. "The FBI, dear!" his wife replied.

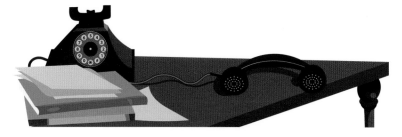

In 1949, Robert embarrassed Lewis Strauss in public at a discussion about atomic energy. Strauss did not want to send certain atomic material to foreign laboratories to help them with their research. Robert disagreed with Strauss and stated at a public meeting that the material should be sent. He joked that the material in question could not be used to create atomic weapons. It was "far less important than electronic devices but far more important than vitamins!" Many people in the room laughed.

When he left the meeting Robert asked a friend, "Did I do well?"

"You did too well," he was told. "You have just made a serious enemy in there."

Strauss was humiliated. He began to plan his revenge. The FBI gave him access to thousands of pages of documents on Robert.

The political scene was now changing in America. Even though they had been allies in the war, the Soviet Union was now regarded as an enemy. People who had supported the Communist Party in the past were now accused of being traitors by politicians like Senator Joe McCarthy.

In 1953, Strauss was appointed the chairperson of the Atomic Energy Commission. Robert still played an important role in this group. Strauss convinced American President Eisenhower that Robert could not be trusted with any secrets. Strauss appointed three people to investigate Robert. Albert Einstein urged Robert to resign. "The trouble with Robert is he loves someone – the United States government – who is not in love with him," he said.

Strauss was now getting daily FBI reports about Robert. They were still listening to him (illegally) at his home and workplace. Robert and his team of lawyers were not allowed to see any reports or documents which accused him of being a spy. By the end of the investigation, Robert's security clearance was removed. Strauss had won. Many scientists disagreed with this decision. As one commentator remarked: "Oppenheimer will no longer have access to secrets in government files. The government will no longer have access to secrets that may be born in Oppenheimer's brain."

Strauss was not finished yet. He tried and failed to remove Robert from his position at the Institute for Advanced Study. When Strauss's actions against Robert were made public in the coming years, he paid a political price as politicians refused to vote for him when he was nominated for a senior government position in 1959.

Years later, Russian security documents confirmed that Robert had never been a spy. In 2022, the decision to remove Oppenheimer's security clearance was overturned by the United Stated government after it was decided that the original ruling decision was "flawed".

Robert's Later Years

While Robert continued his role at the Institute, he and his family started to spend time at his beach house on Saint John's Island in the U.S. Virgin Islands. He helped to establish the World Academy of Art and Science with Albert Einstein and other notable scientists and academics. He also travelled around the world giving lectures.

In 1963, the American president Lyndon Johnson presented Robert with an important scientific award for "his contribution to physics and the advancement of science." Robert thanked the president for his "charity and courage" in making this award.

Robert passed away in his sleep at Princeton on 18th February 1967 at the age of sixty-two. His body was cremated, and his ashes were dropped into the sea near his house on Saint John's Island.

Fellow scientists paid tribute to Robert after his passing. They said he was "a great leader of science in our time, one of the most remarkable personalities of the century who will leave a lasting memory. He had a truly brilliant mind and always gave you the answer before you had the time to prepare the question!"

The Survivors of the Atomic Bomb

In 1960 Robert travelled to Japan for a series of lectures. At a gathering in Osaka, he was handed a letter that invited him to Hiroshima. It said: *"Hiroshima citizens bear no animosity towards any individual for the tragedy which overtook them ... their only hope is that there will never be another Hiroshima."* Robert never had the chance to visit the city.

Atomic weapons and testing had many long-term impacts on people, not only in Japan but around the world.

In the United States, people who lived in New Mexico saw the bright lights of the "Trinity" test in 1945. They were told it was nothing to worry about – some ammunition had blown up accidentally. When it became clear that people (and animals on farms) near these tests had fallen sick due to radioactive fallout, the American government had to provide financial compensation. These people became known as "downwinders" because they lived downwind from the test site. Many of the people who lived next to the "Trinity" site became very ill in the years after the testing.

In Hiroshima and Nagasaki there were many stories of heroic survival.

Flight Lieutenant Joseph Aidan McCarthy from Cork was in a Japanese prisoner-of-war camp in Nagasaki when the bomb was dropped. The camp was destroyed. Joseph survived after running into a bomb shelter. As he was a doctor, he tried to help the wounded people. He did not suffer any after-effects and lived into his eighties.

A group of brave Japanese survivors known as the *hibakusha* began to share their experiences. Their stories of perseverance and resilience were told around the world.

Tsutomu Yamaguchi survived both the Hiroshima and Nagasaki bombings. At the age of twenty-nine he had just completed a business trip to Hiroshima and was preparing to travel back to his hometown of Nagasaki when the bomb fell. He suffered burns and damage to his eardrums but managed to get a train to Nagasaki. He reported for work at his Nagasaki office after receiving hospital treatment. Just as he was telling his colleagues about the Hiroshima bomb, the second bomb detonated. "I thought the mushroom cloud had followed me," he told a newspaper reporter years later. He suffered radiation poisoning but recovered and lived into his nineties.

Taeko Teramae was fifteen years old and trapped in a building that was on fire in Hiroshima after the bomb was dropped. She jumped out of a second-storey window and climbed down a telephone pole to escape. Her face became very swollen and she began to lose her sight. Taeko's schoolteacher helped her to swim across a river to safety just as Taeko lost her sight completely. Taeko recovered her sight eventually. Years later, at the age of ninety, she had a message for the peoples of the world: "I hope people around the world will be considerate to each other and take a step toward a world without war."

Setsuko Thurlow was in Hiroshima. She was thirteen years old. After seeing a blinding bluish-white flash, Setsuko was thrown through the air with the impact of the explosion. She lost consciousness. When she woke up, she was trapped in the rubble and could not move. It was very dark. Hands touched her left shoulder, and she heard a voice saying "*Don't give up, keep pushing! I am trying to free you. See the light coming through that opening? Crawl towards it as quickly as you can!*" Setsuko escaped and survived.

In 2017, the United Nations outlawed the development and testing of nuclear weapons. The International Campaign to Abolish Nuclear Weapons (ICAN) won the Nobel Peace Prize that year. Setsuko was a member of this group.

At the awards ceremony, Setsuko shared her experiences and spoke of her hopes for the abolition of nuclear weapons: "I want you to feel the presence of all those who perished in Hiroshima and Nagasaki. Each person had a name. Each person was loved by someone. Let us ensure their deaths were not in vain. In Hiroshima I kept pushing towards the light to survive. The light we seek now is a ban on nuclear weapons. To all in this hall and all listening around the world, I repeat those words that I heard called to me in the ruins of Hiroshima: *'Don't give up! Keep pushing! See the light? Crawl towards it!'*"

Glossary

Bellyaching: Complaining.

Black Hole: A giant star that ran out of energy and collapsed within itself.

Chemistry: A part of science that looks at chemical elements and compounds.

Communism: A movement to create a society where everything is shared by the people. However, the Communist Party in the Soviet Union under Joseph Stalin did not create an equal society.

Federal Bureau of Investigation (FBI): A security organisation whose role is to protect the American people and uphold the Constitution of the USA.

Hindu: The world's third largest religion, mainly practised in Southeast Asia.

Nuclear Countries: Eight countries in the world have nuclear weapons today: China, France, India, North Korea, Pakistan, Russia, United Kingdom, and the USA. (It is understood that Israel has nuclear weapons but has not publicly declared that it has.)

Ph.D. (Doctor of Philosophy): Highest qualification a student can get in third-level education.

Physics: A part of science that looks at physical objects and the forces that act to pull or push on these objects.

Sheila Power: Lecturer at University College Dublin, teaching mathematical courses. In 1941, she was the first Irishwoman to receive a Ph.D. in Mathematics.

Soviet Union: Union of Socialist Republics which existed between 1922 until 1991. Russia was the largest member.

World Academy of Art and Science: Founded by Robert Oppenheimer, Albert Einstein and others in 1960 to discuss the challenges that face humanity and help to change the world for the better.

Some Things to Talk About

1. Where did Robert live?

2. Who were his parents?

3. What was Robert's favourite hobby?

4. Where did Robert study?

5. What did Robert teach?

6. What was the Great Depression?

7. Why did Albert Einstein write a letter to President Roosevelt?

8. What was The Manhattan Project?

9. What four cities were chosen as targets for the atomic bomb?

10. Which two cities were bombed?

11. Why did the FBI investigate Robert?

12. How many children did Robert and his wife Kitty have?

13. Where did Robert start to spend time after he lost his security clearance?

14. What special award did Robert receive in 1963?

15. What decision did the U.S. government make in 1922?

Timeline

1904:   Julius Robert born in New York City. He calls himself Robert.

1911:   Goes to the Ethical Cultural School in New York City.

1922:   Attends Harvard University. Discovers Los Alamos School while horse-riding in New Mexico.

1927:   Receives a doctorate in Physics at the University of Gottingen in Germany.

1928:   Begins teaching at the California Institute of Technology (Caltech).

1929:   Begins a second teaching role at the University of California (Berkeley).

1938:   Lise Meitner, Otto Hahn and Fritz Strassman successfully split the atom.

1939:   World War Two begins after the Nazis invade Poland.
Einstein writes his letter to President Roosevelt.

1940:   Robert marries Katherine "Kitty" Puening.

1941:   Japan attacks Pearl Harbour in December. USA now enters the war.
Peter Oppenheimer born.

1942:   Robert becomes involved in Manhattan Project to create the atomic bomb.

1944:   Katherine "Toni" Oppenheimer born.

1945:   Nazis surrender in June.
President Roosevelt dies. Harry Truman becomes American President.
Atomic bombs dropped on Hiroshima and Nagasaki.
Japan surrenders in August. World War Two ends.
Robert argues against creation of hydrogen bomb.

1947:   Robert appointed Director of Institute for Advanced Study in Princeton, New Jersey.

1953:   Dwight D. Eisenhower becomes President of the USA.

1954:   Loses Security Clearance.

1963:   Awarded the Enrico Fermi Award by President Johnson.

1967:   Dies in Princeton, New Jersey.

2022:   United States government announces Robert's security clearance should not have been removed.